MEMORY THEATRE

Simon Critchley is Hans Jonas Professor of Philosophy at the New School for Social Research in New York. His previous books include *On Humour*, *The Book of Dead Philosophers*, *How to Stop Living and Start Worrying*, *Impossible Objects*, *The Mattering of Matter* (with Tom McCarthy), *The Faith of the Faithless*, *Stay, Illusion!: The Hamlet Doctrine* (with Jamieson Webster), *Bowie*, and *Notes on Suicide* (also published by Fitzcarraldo Editions). He is series moderator of 'The Stone', a philosophy column in the *New York Times*, to which he is a frequent contributor.

Liam Gillick is a British artist based in New York. He was nominated for the Turner Prize in 2002, represented Germany for the 53rd Venice Biennale in 2009, and has taught at Columbia University since 1997. Public collections include: Government Art Collection, UK; Arts Council, UK; Tate, London; Museum of Modern Art, New York; Guggenheim Museum, New York; Hirshhorn Museum, Washington DC; Museum of Contemporary Art, Chicago.

'With a sense of mischief combined with surprising reverie, Simon Critchley has braided together ideas about memory from the past with the latest thinking about unreliable narrative, altered states and the mysteries of consciousness. *Memory Theatre* is a tantalising, textual Moebius strip – philosophy, autobiography and fiction twisted together.'
— Marina Warner, author of *Stranger Magic*

'Simon Critchley is a figure of quite startling brilliance, and I can never begin to guess what he'll do next, only that it is sure to sustain and nourish my appetite for his voice. His overall project may be that of returning philosophical inquiry, and "theory", to a home in literature, yet without surrendering any of its incisive power, or ethical urgency. ... I read *Memory Theatre* and loved it.'
— Jonathan Lethem, author of *Dissident Gardens*

'Novella or essay, science-fiction or memoir? Who cares. Chris Marker, Adolfo Bioy Casares and Frances Yates would all have been proud to have written *Memory Theatre*.'
— Tom McCarthy, author of *C*

'A strange, affecting and stimulating book that's both a philosophical history and a personal memoir. Sifting through the archives of a dead friend, Critchley takes a fascinating journey through the philosophy and history of memory, and the technologies of remembering dreamed up by thinkers since classical times.'
— Hari Kunzru, author of *Gods Without Men*

'This is a remarkable [fiction] debut: rich, profound and clever, but not oppressively so, and often very funny.'
— Nicholas Lezard, *Guardian*

Fitzcarraldo Editions

MEMORY THEATRE

SIMON CRITCHLEY

Images by
LIAM GILLICK

¶ I was dying. That much was certain. The rest is fiction.

The fear of death slept for most of the day and then crept up late at night and grabbed me by the throat, making sleep impossible no matter how much alcohol I had drunk that evening. Insomnia had been my clandestine companion for much of my adult life, at least after the accident. But since the discovery of the boxes and the building of the memory theatre, it had intensified with the force of an implacable logic: If I was going to die anyway, then why sleep?

Then the bladder game would begin. Teeth brushed and flossed, a confident final piss in the toilet, a few pages of *Ulysses* perused in the exquisite 1960 cloth-bound Bodley Head edition, sleep would softly descend... only to be interrupted by that vague alien-like pressure in the lower abdomen. Do I need to piss or don't I? Up and down, to and fro, throughout the night until the terrors of darkness disappeared with dawn. Suicidal and sometimes homicidal thoughts would slowly subside. Sleep would come, but too late.

The next day I would walk around with a thousand invisible tiny lacerations around the eyes and a painfully acute sensitivity to noise that would make the most humdrum tasks hugely cumbersome. This had gone on for three years, my fear growing stronger ever since the realization. I was exhausted with exhaustion.

¶ I had moved from England to New York in January 2004 to see if my necronautical activities met with a kinder reception in the New World than the indifference I had experienced in the old one. On return to the University of Essex that June, in an effort to clear up and leave my old office, sort through my papers and finally move my books, a peculiar thing happened.

Semi-hidden in my office, I came across an unfamiliar series of boxes, five of them in a stack, sort of mid-sized, brown cardboard boxes. After speaking to Barbara, the administrator in the philosophy department, it became clear that they were the unpublished papers, notes and remains of a close friend and former philosophy teacher of mine in France, Michel Haar. They had been sent unannounced by his brother from the sanatorium in which Michel died from a heart attack in the dreadful summer heatwave that swept France in 2003. His death had followed a long bout of neurological, psychological and hypochondriacal illnesses that had besieged him since taking early retirement from his chair in the philosophy department at the Sorbonne and which, indeed, were the cause of his early retirement. Truth to tell, there was always a slightly maniacal death wish in Michel. When he finally received his chair in Paris, the dream of every self-respecting French academic, he incorrectly told everyone he was replacing Sarah Kofman, the great Nietzsche scholar, who had committed suicide on the 150th anniversary of Nietzsche's birth. Michel seemed determined to repeat the fate of his supposed predecessor.

I subsequently tried to contact Michel's brother Roger, whom I'd met once for dinner in a terrible chain restaurant in Paris ('Hippopotamus' or something like that; Michel was a cheapskate and didn't care about food). I had his phone number in Strasbourg, but it no longer worked. I sent a letter that was later returned unopened, 'retour à l'envoyeur' stamped across it. Michel was divorced and estranged from his wife, Anne, after refusing to have children. Narcissistic to the end. I knew of no other immediate family members. I was left with the perplexity of not knowing why these boxes had been sent to me. Michel had a few devoted students who knew him much better than I did. He didn't really have what you would call friends.

I immediately began to go through the boxes, finding everything within them in apparent disorder, although each box was marked with a sign of the zodiac, from Capricorn to Gemini. The Taurus box was missing. Had it been lost in transit or was there some design at work? The *zodiacal* signs didn't surprise me as Michel was possibly the first philosopher since Pico della Mirandola in the late fifteenth century to have a deep commitment to astrology. Like Pico, Michel was a genethlialogist, a maker of horoscopes.

In the box marked Capricorn, I found some absolute gems, such as notes from a lecture on ethics and Marxism by Jean-Paul Sartre at the École normale supérieur in 1959, when Michel was a student. There was also the transcription of a debate between Sartre and several *normaliens*, including two of my former teachers, Clément Rosset and Dominique Janicaud, and a young, vital and very Sartrean Alain Badiou. I found 'Notes de cours' from Louis Althusser's class on materialism in ancient philosophy, with long discussions of Leucippus, Democritus, Epicurus and Lucretius.

To my complete astonishment, I found the original copies of a triangular correspondence between Jean Beaufret, Jacques Lacan and Martin Heidegger, which concerned the latter's visit to Cerisy-la-Salle near

Saint-Lô in Normandy in 1955 to deliver the lecture, 'Was ist das – die Philosophie?', the title of which had always made me laugh. Don't know why. Most amusingly, some of the correspondence between Lacan and Beaufret deals with the topic of what Herr *und* Frau Heidegger might choose to eat for breakfast *chez* Lacan during their passage through Paris. Lacan had made complex plans to obtain specially imported *Schwarzbrot* from Alsace, together with hard cheeses and ham. Beaufret spends some paragraphs reassuring Lacan that the Heideggers looked forward to nothing better than some croissants, a café crème and perhaps a little *tartine*. Beaufret, a tortured, closeted homosexual who spent most of his days in his pyjamas, was in analysis with Lacan for five years and this was the only time that the great psychoanalyst ever appeared to take any interest in him.

I found a large number of more conventional academic manuscripts in the first box, which kept circling back to the problem of nihilism and to Michel's lifelong fascination with Heidegger's mighty two-volume *Nietzsche*, based on lectures from the late 1930s, but which had appeared in German in 1961 when Michel was in his early twenties. Heidegger himself and many of his apologists saw these lectures as the place where a critique of National Socialist ideology was being articulated after his fateful and hateful tenure as Rector of Freiburg University for about a year from the time the Nazis came to power in 1933. I thought that such apologetics were bullshit. For Michel, much more interestingly, what was at stake was the question of the relation between philosophy and poetry, in particular the disclosive possibilities of non-propositional forms of language such as verbalized nouns and tautologies. To what extent was Nietzsche's wildly inventive, poetic and polemical thinking contained by Heidegger's increasingly strident philosophical critique, which interpreted Nietzsche as the mere inversion of Plato and, ultimately, as a figure for our entrapment in metaphysical modes of thinking, rather than a release from them? On this reading, Nietzsche was not the exit from nihilism, but its highest expression, its fulfilment. (There was a German word for this – there always is – but I've forgotten it.)

Michel kept coming back, in text after text, to the poetic dimension of Nietzsche's language and style as that which might escape philosophy. This line of argument was continued in a series of extraordinary short hand-written papers I found on various poets: Saint-John Perse (Michel had introduced me to his long poem, *Anabase*, when I first met him – I still read it in T. S. Eliot's translation), Francis Ponge (an essay on the descriptive prose poems in *Le parti pris des choses*), Wallace Stevens (on his late poems from 'The Rock' – he had discovered Stevens through Anne) and Rilke's 'Ninth Duino Elegy' (a commentary on the words, 'Praise this world to the angel, not the unsayable'). On each occasion, he showed, with exquisite delicacy, the fragile force of poetic language as that which pushes back against hard reality and pulls free of flat-footed philosophy.

Poetry lets us see things as they are. It lets us see particulars being various. But – Michel insisted – poetry lets us see things as they are anew. Under a new aspect. Transfigured. Subject to a felt variation. The poet sings a song that is beyond us and yet it is ourselves that it sings. Things change when the poet sings them, but they are still our things: recognizable, common, near, low. We hear the poet sing and press back against the pressure of reality. I instantly thought that many of these texts could have been published, if I could interest the increasingly

13

flagging and beleaguered French and Anglophone academic presses. But such plans soon seemed irrelevant.

Michel had a small cult following in France and the United States, but lacked the capacity for endless and shameless self-promotion that most often defines philosophical fame. He slipped into his pyjamas around 10.30 p.m. and slept like the dead thanks to the chemical kindness of his liberal doctor. While sometimes spotted with moments of brilliance, Michel's talks in English were usually long, rambling and incoherent. He also often seemed to lose interest in what he was saying.

In the Aquarius box, I found many strange maps. Michel had somehow obtained an annotated cloth print of the Mappa Mundi from Hereford Cathedral. This extraordinary object from around 1300 presents the world divided into three continents (Europe, Asia, Africa), with its centre in Jerusalem, which was shaped like a little keyhole. I came across a series of almost fantastical antique maps of Australia or more precisely New Holland, seemingly drawn by French explorers from the early to mid-1700s. There were hand-drawn maps of the estuarial systems of Virginia and North Carolina, combined with exhaustive descriptions of flora and fauna. Most impressive of all was Michel's own six feet by four map of natural catastrophe, with extensive detail on the paths of hurricanes in the Caribbean and the Gulf of Mexico, the tornadoes of the American Midwest, maps of volcanic explosions from Vesuvius to Krakatoa and beyond. There was also a detailed prose description of the meteorite the size of Manhattan that allegedly fell on the Yucatán Peninsula fifteen million years ago, wiping out most forms of life on earth, including all dinosaur species.

In the Gemini box, I discovered heavily annotated

copies of Marsilio Ficino's translations of Plato, especially *The Symposium*, and Tommaso Campanella's *City of the Sun*. (Michel was obsessed with the description of the ideal city with its religion based on a solar cult. Oddly, when we were together in Italy in those summers, he always avoided the sun.) I also found a series of fragmentary but fascinating drafts for a study of the technological metaphors in Heidegger's *Sein und Zeit*, with deeply original insights on Heidegger's obvious references to hands, hammers, nails and the workshop world of fundamental ontology, but less obvious references to car indicators, washing machines, typewriters, radio signals and even primitive computer systems: 'For there too the gods are present,' Heidegger would seem to be suggesting. I came across transcribed notes from a number of sessions of a Heidegger reading group that took place informally at the ENS in the early 1960s and which included Michel, his great friend Dominique Janicaud and a young Jacques Derrida, as well as a number of visiting Americans. I remember Michel telling me about this group, which was almost covert and against the grain during the overwhelming hegemony in Paris in those years of what was called 'le freudo-marxisme'.

In Gemini, I also found a short, odd text – written in English – called, 'The One True Philosophy of Clothes'. It was anonymous, but my guess is that it was written by Michel's American wife, Anne, who worked for many years in the Paris fashion industry, a job that she had great difficulty combining with her immense passion for Ibsen, Racine and Attic tragedy, especially Euripides. The consequence of this collision was satire and the model was Thomas Carlyle's *Sartor Resartus*, 'The Tailor Retailored'. She begins by writing:

What is the human being but a garment and what is the world but the living garment of God? If language is the expressive garment of thought, then clothes are the expressive garment of the body. Nature and life itself is but one garment woven and ever-weaving from the loom of time. As Carlyle writes, 'The whole external universe and what holds it together is but clothing and the essence of all science lies in the PHILOSOPHY OF CLOTHES.'

The philosophy of clothes is not some specialized sub-discipline taught in fashion schools. It is the key to understanding everything. It is the germ and gem of all science. The human being is the fashioned animal and fashion is the key to understanding the human being. Let me put this in a simple linguistic formula: Mankind = manikin = mannequin. Like Plato's demiurge or creator-deity in the *Timaeus*, the fashion designer takes the old rags of matter and forms them into something sublime. God is the great fashion designer in the sky and the fashion designers here on earth are his prophets, his true disciples: mortal portals to his immortal power.

Not bad. My mind wandered. I thought of Adam and Eve after the Fall, discovering their nakedness and clothing themselves. Were they naked before the Fall? No. They may have been nude, but not naked. For they wore the garment of God's grace, the radiant garment of glory. With the exit from Paradise, to cover our shame, we wear either the penitential skins of wild animals or the many-coloured robes of vanity. But this is mortuary clothing, funereal dress until we put on the white robes of baptism. I looked down at my feet. Did they wear flip-flops in Paradise?

My first job was working as a researcher in what used

16

to be called University College Cardiff for a prominent biologist, Russell Lloyd; I suppose that today he would be called a neuroscientist. He had become obsessed with the history of research on the nervous system and needed a humanist who could do archive work. It was infinitely dull, but I got paid and it led me to Freud's early research on the testicles of eels and Georg Büchner's paper on the skull nerves of fish, and from there into his dramatic works, particularly *Danton's Death*. Prophetic.

When in Cardiff I received a handwritten letter from Michel telling me that his wife had left him for an English civil engineer. She was living somewhere in South Wales and having a tough time. Apparently, she had become enamoured with the engineer (whom I never met – was he called Simon?) during choir practice in an Anglican church in Paris. How odd. Anne and I met on a few occasions and had some memorable long walks in the countryside outside Cardiff, where she lived, usually in drizzle. She explained in an astonished, French-inflected, New England, Anne Sexton-like accent that her new neighbours had not even heard of *Anna Karenina*, let alone read it. Can you imagine? During the last of those walks, she was visibly pregnant. I left Cardiff soon afterwards for my first teaching post and we completely lost touch. I think she changed her name. I often think about that child.

¶ Nothing had prepared me for what I found in the Aries box. Michel had written a long text, written around 1967 or '68, on Hegel called 'Le théâtre de mémoire selon G. W. F. Hegel', an entirely original interpretation of Hegel's monumental 1807 *Phenomenology of Spirit*. The basic idea of the memory theatre was borrowed from the highly influential writings of the London-based art historian Frances Yates and in particular her 1966 book, *The Art of Memory*.

Anglophile that he was, Michel had obviously read the book shortly after it had been published in London. Curiously, it just so happened that I read this book very closely during the summer of 1986, around the time I first met Michel in Italy, and had even tried to adapt some of its ideas on Leibniz's project for a 'general characteristic' into an essay I was trying to write on the history of the idea of a universal language, so beautifully ridiculed by Swift in book three of *Gulliver's Travels*, the voyage to the academy of Laputa. Artificial memory machines litter history. Human beings seem to be persistently seduced by the idea that a theatre, a palace or a machine might be constructed that would hold the sum of knowledge in a way that would permit total recall. All we would need to do in order to attain absolute knowledge would be to enter the theatre or machine and commit to memory everything therein. Of course, given what happened, it is easy to say that now.

Yates tries to show how a counter-history of the occident can be traced through the cultivation of mnemotechnic systems, the textual basis for which can be traced back at least as far as Socrates' denunciation of writing as a form of artificial, external memory in the *Phaedrus*. The idea begins with the ancient Greek poet, Simonides, who was reciting a poem in a house when the ceiling

18

collapsed. Somehow he escaped, although everybody else was crushed to death. Although the bodies of the victims were unrecognizably mangled by the gravity of the fall, Simonides was able to recall the precise places where the guests were sitting. With the association of memory with locus and location, the idea of a memory house, memory palace or memory theatre was born. The time of speech could be mastered by the spatial recollections of *loci*, of *topoi*. One would walk around in one's memory as if in a building or, better, storehouse, inspecting the objects therein. Saint Augustine, trained as a teacher of rhetoric, even went looking for God in memory, only to discover there was 'no place' where he could be found.

Very singular is this art of the memory theatre. Records suggest that the construction of such theatres in antiquity reflected the proportions of classical architecture, but in an unclassical spirit, concentrating their choices on irregular places and avoiding symmetrical orders. They were full of human imagery, active and dramatic, beautiful or grotesque. In all cases, memorable. They remind one more of figures in some Gothic cathedral rather than classical art proper. Appearing utterly amoral, the purpose of the images is to give an emotional impetus to memory by means of their idiosyncrasy or strangeness. This kind of artificial memory was common in antiquity. Seneca, a teacher of rhetoric, could recite 2,000 names in the order in which they had been given. Simplicius, a friend of Saint Augustine, could recite Virgil backwards. (I once met a Swede at a party in Stockholm who could sing every Swedish entry to the Eurovision Song Contest since 1958 – you just said the year, 1978 say, and he would begin: 'Dinga, dinga dong/Binga, binga bong.') The striking images in a memory theatre would arouse intense inner powers of visualization to aid recollection.

There was always an ancient connection between the art of memory and forms of occult Hermeticism, especially astrology. Metrodorus of Scepsis is said to have written on the order of the images of the zodiac all that he wanted to remember. But Yates shows how this ancient memory tradition is powerfully reanimated in the classicism and occultism of the Italian Renaissance. Marsilio Ficino, the translator of Plato into Latin, also translated the *Corpus Hermeticum* and the dialogues with Hermes Trismegistus. When the art of memory met the new teachings of the Renaissance with their belief in the divinity of man, then recollection became the *via regia* for recalling the entirety of knowledge from its first principles. With the mastery of the right techniques of memory, total recall would be possible and the human would become divine. The memory theatre was the microcosm of the divine macrocosm of the universe.

The Renaissance memory theatre announces a novel juncture in the history of memory. The architecture is no longer the Gothic cathedral by which the human creature might recall the totality of God's creation, from the Fall to incarnation and resurrection through to the Last Judgement. On the contrary, the mind and memory of man are divine, having the powers of grasping the highest reality through a magically activated imagination. The art of memory becomes a Hermetic, occult and implicitly heretical art. For the Catholic Church, incarnation is not a two-way street.

The most audacious and, indeed, memorable version of a Renaissance memory theatre is that of Giulio Camillo Delminio, who was born around 1480. Although facts are scarce, Camillo reportedly built a small wooden version of his memory theatre in Venice, which various luminaries visited. In a letter to Erasmus, Viglius Zuichemus writes,

'They say that Giulio Camillo has constructed a certain Amphitheatre, a work of wonderful skill, in which whoever is admitted as spectator will be able to discourse on any subject no less fluently than Cicero.' The eminently rational Erasmus was not amused.

In 1530, Camillo went to Paris at the request of King Francis I of France. He had been given a large pension in order to build a full-scale version of the memory theatre. It was never finished, although there were reports of various maquettes being produced. In 1554, after Camillo's death, a manuscript was published in Venice with the title *L'Idea del Theatro dell'eccellen. M. Giulio Camillo*. The text gives a prose description of the proposed theatre divided into seven chapters, which describe the nature of the seven grades or steps of the theatre. Yates produced a detailed two-dimensional schema of the theatre where the seven steps are intersected by seven gangways representing the seven planets. The normal theatre function is reversed. The solitary spectator of the spectacle stands onstage gazing at the images in the auditorium. As in ancient theatres, the most distinguished guests sat at the front, the most important items of recollection would be in the lowest place in the theatre, 'il primo grado del Theatro'.

The theatre in some ways resembles a vast and highly ornamental filing cabinet. The auditorium of the wooden theatre was filled with many various and striking figures bedecked with seemingly obscure details and decorations: some symbols simply reflected the elements of the *trivium* and *quadrivium* that constituted the canon of the liberal arts. But other symbols were more obscure: a blindfolded woman standing on a serpent bearing scales in one hand denoted the various elements of natural law and its triumph over criminality; a bloodied pelican represented the mystery of the Eucharist and a reminder of the doctrine of Christ's *kenosis*; and so on. Interestingly, the theatre was circular and globe-like. It recalled the Vitruvian circle that circumscribes the perfection of human form which is itself an image and reflection of the cosmos. On this view, the very idea of theatre, at the core of the Italian Renaissance with the construction of the Teatro Olimpico in Vicenza in the 1580s, is heresy: the unity of the human and the divine.

¶ The ancient art of memory found its most powerful advocate in the formidable personage of Giordano Bruno, born in 1548. If Copernicus ignited a revolution in astronomy and our entire thinking about the universe, then it was Bruno who spread that fire all across Europe and who was finally engulfed by the conflagration. His theories of an infinite universe and a multiplicity of worlds, combined with his fascination with the Hermetic tradition of magic and the arts of memory, led to multiple charges of heresy.

Following his excommunication in Italy and an accusation of murder, Giordano Bruno settled for a time in Paris, London, Oxford and various university towns in Germany. In 1591, he made the fatal move of returning to Italy, where he was tried for heresy, briefly in Venice and for seven long years in Rome. After being condemned to death for refusing to retract his views, he famously said to his judges, 'Perhaps your fear in passing judgement on me is greater than mine in receiving it.' He was gagged and burned alive on the Campo de Fiori. Bruno has also always been seen as the dissenting enemy of a repressive Catholic Church. In many small Italian towns the Piazza Giordano Bruno stands directly opposite the main Catholic Church, often at the initiative of the local Communist Party.

Bruno was the Simon Magus figure of a Hermetic tradition of the arts of memory. In Frances Yates's words, its central doctrine is, 'All is in all in nature. So in the intellect all is in all. And memory can memorize all in all.'

Through techniques of memory, the human being can achieve absolute knowledge and become divine. For Bruno, to understand is to speculate with images, where the human mind is the mirror of the cosmos which functions through powerful, proto-Jungian archetypes.

Through the divine power of the imagination, the intellect can seize hold of the whole.

Bruno's art of memory is enshrined in texts like *Torch of the Thirty Statues* from 1558, where towering mythological statues embody a Michelangelesque memory: Apollo, naked in his chariot, his head nimbed with solar rays, is the Monad or One; Saturn, brandishing his sickle, is the Beginning or Time; Minerva is the divine in man reflecting the divine universe; the infigurable Orcus or Abyss signifies the thirst for divine infinity.

Bruno was an occupant of the French Embassy in London from 1583-86, the key years for the Renaissance in English poetry, ushered in by Sir Philip Sidney, Fulke Greville, and his group. These people were close to Bruno during his London years and he also met with John Dee, the Hermetic philosopher and astrologer to Queen Elizabeth, who was the teacher of Sidney and Greville. Indeed, some believe that Greville was the author of plays attributed to Shakespeare, some of which were lost. Although such speculations are dubious, there is documentary evidence connecting Greville to Shakespeare and indeed mentioning that the former was the latter's 'master' (they both hailed from Warwickshire). Maybe the young Will found admittance into the circles of the Hermetic art of memory.

Such speculations find some anchor in history if we consider the writings of another Hermetic philosopher of the period, Robert Fludd. One of Yates's most far-reaching contentions in *The Art of Memory* is that the memory space described in Fludd's obscure treatises on the two worlds (the *Utriusque Cosmi*), and which he describes as 'public theatres', may reflect or even anticipate the circular architecture of Shakespeare's Globe Theatre.

Is it not at least plausible to speculate that the Globe

Theatre, with its heavens over part of the stage, complete with zodiacal symbols, was not some adapted bear pit or inn yard as is commonly thought, but an elaborate and geometrically exacting theatre of memory, a kind of machine for recalling the whole, a mortal portal for touching the divine, a microcosm for the cosmic macrocosm? Shakespearean theatre might thus be the continuation of ancient and Renaissance traditions of the art of memory, a concrete building that embodied the operations of occult memory. If 'All the world's a stage', then the theatre is the stage of the world itself: its mirror and key.

26

¶ The wilder excesses of Yates's book fascinated me in the mid-1980s, as they had attracted Michel in the late 1960s. For example, the idea that there might be a connection between the 'Giordanisti' (the followers of Bruno) and the Rosicrucians, the mysterious brotherhood of the Rosy Cross announced by manifestos published in Germany in the early 1600s and which might never have existed, and with the Freemasons, who first surface in 1646 in England. The speculative masonry of this cult, with its emphasis on architecture and building, is also a tributary of the art of memory.

Yates ends her book by claiming that the art of memory does not disappear with Elizabethan theatre, but reappears in a more secular and respectable guise in the various seventeenth century projects for an encyclopedia of knowledge that would reflect the world and make it available to memory. We find such projects in Bacon, Descartes and Leibniz – indeed, Leibniz took over the concept of the 'Monad' from Bruno.

The seventeenth-century fascination with the idea of a universal language, stimulated by Bacon's demand for 'real characters' for expressing notions, comes straight out of the tradition of the art of memory and is a rationalization of the occult and magical memory images of Bruno. This led to Leibniz's plans for a 'characteristica': a system of universal signs based on the invention of infinitesimal calculus, a kind of modern hieroglyphics, an attempted recovery of the language of Adam against the Babel of the world. These signs would be placed onto a vast combinatorial machine, a proto-computer, the calculations of which would provide all possible permutations of the knowable.

Like Camillo's stupendous memory theatre, Leibniz never completed his plan for the universal characteristic and ended his life in failure, an unwanted and ignored courtier abandoned by his patron Duke George Ludwig, who went off to become King of England in 1714, leaving Leibniz in Hannover. But their *hybris* lives on in the idea of a universal key, a *clavisuniversalis*, that would unlock the secrets of nature, an arcane encyclopedia that would arrive at universal knowledge through the right combination of the constituent, abstracted features of reality. And what subtends this desire for an encyclopedia, Yates contends, is an ecumenical drive for an ethic of universal love and charity that would overcome all the religious differences that lead to intolerance and war, a kind of Rosicrucian effort at a universal reformation of man, the occult humanist strand at the heart of the Northern European Enlightenment.

¶ Michel's simple but brilliant idea was to read Hegel's *Phenomenology of Spirit* as a memory theatre, namely as a continuation of Yates's tradition of the art of memory. The main protagonist in Hegel's book – the book that nearly ruined my life when I first read it at the age of 23 (I thought it was too incontestably true and it ruined everything else I read) – is a personage called Geist or Spirit. By Spirit, Hegel means no less than the entire cultural development of the world. His basic thought is that Spirit requires a series of appearances or phenomena in arresting, dramatic and memorable images. These images, or what Hegel calls 'shapes', by which world history is traced as if in silhouette, have to be seized by the self and made our own. The stated goal of Hegel's philosophy is that substance becomes subject: namely that the knowledge of the whole which exists externally in its historical movement has to be grasped internally by the self. This is the process of education whereby a self ascends to an experience of self-determination.

This grasping of the whole is what Hegel calls 'absolute knowledge' and he insists that this is only possible as recollection. This is why Hegel fills his book with vivid and indeed bloody images, such as the life-and-death struggle between master and slave, the unhappy consciousness, the vapidly legislating Stoic, the beautiful soul made mad by the world, and the terroristic reign of virtue in the French Revolution, where death had no more meaning than cutting the head off a cabbage or swallowing a gulp of water. Hegel's pages are full of exaggerated and powerfully visual images, aides to recollection, like Bruno's statues or the icons in the seats of Camillo's theatre. The *Phenomenology of Spirit* is a memory theatre where the long path of the world's historical development can be held in the storehouse of memory and obsessively replayed. Hegel insists that the movement of Spirit is the circle that returns into itself, a circle that presupposes its beginning and reaches it only at the end. The theatre of Spirit is a globe.

Hegel's philosophy is a mnemotechnic system in the ancient and Renaissance tradition. The difference is that what Hegel adds to his memory theatre is time, that is, the experience of becoming. Rather than the static ensemble of Camillo, Hegel's is a moving theatre, a kind of proto-cinema. In the final paragraph of the *Phenomenology of Spirit*, Hegel talks of becoming as a slow-moving succession of spirits, a gallery of images, each endowed with all the riches of Spirit, moving slowly so that the self can penetrate and digest the entire wealth of its substance. This is why the *Phenomenology* can only be read in reverse. It's like driving a car while constantly looking in the rearview mirror.

The German *Erinnerung* denotes both recollection and the active experience of making inward. As such, it can be opposed to forms of external, mechanical, technologized or even neuro-physiological memory, captured in the word *Gedächtnis*. The Hegelian art of memory is the inwardizing of all the shapes of Spirit. In memory, the whole world of history is emptied into subjectivity, filling up the void of the self. This fulfilment is what is meant by absolute knowledge: the unity of divine and the human, what Hegel calls in the final words of the book, 'The Calvary of absolute Spirit'.

Absolute knowledge is the final shape of Spirit, the end that returns to the beginning where the movie show begins again, and again, and again. Repetition, repetition, repetition – I thought of Mark E. Smith of the mighty Fall. Perhaps the task of each subsequent generation would be the construction of its own living memory theatre, its own construction of the past in thought and image. The difference from Camillo's theatre, which has the subject onstage and the items to be remembered filling the auditorium, is that in Hegel's theatre the subject sits in an auditorium alone and views the shapes of Spirit passing onstage in succession on a vast reel, trying to recall them all. For Hegel, what is being recalled is the history of Spirit, namely the very history that implicitly constitutes the viewing subject. What happens onstage is the entire spiritual drama of subjectivity, our drama. Through the art of memory, we learn to see ourselves from the perspective of the whole, from the standpoint of totality. In so doing, we become infinite, divinely human.

¶ Michel's essay was astonishing, far and away the best thing I'd ever read by him. I had no idea why he didn't publish it. It was admittedly the sketch of a larger argument. Maybe he moved on or just lost interest. Typical of him. However, I found the idea of a memory theatre, even the Hegelian version, slightly droll, as I had lost much of my memory after the accident. All I remembered from that morning in the pharmaceutical factory was Jilted John playing on the radio – 'Gordon is a moron' – and blood all over the floor. I loved that song. It was even more stripped down than conventional punk: two chords instead of three. Then my hand got trapped in the machine by inch-thick steel paddles. Steel slicing flesh. After I pulled out my hand, horribly mangled and hanging by bloody tendons and shards of bone, I collapsed.

I remember being blissfully out of my brain on Pethidine in a hospital bed and trying to put my hand up a nurse's skirt. Then I blacked out. Then I remember going into the operating theatre. I blacked out again. My dad was by my bedside as I came round, my hand suspended above me and wrapped in vast bandages. It was dark and I told him that it wasn't my fault this time. Then I lost consciousness again.

After three operations and as many weeks in hospital, I was told by the specialist that my hand wouldn't have to be amputated. Here it is in front of me right now, arthritic and disfigured with a huge skin-graft scar, but still capable of slow two-finger typing. Tap, tap. A registered disability, no less. It's like that bloody short story by Maupassant. I kept my hand, more or less, but lost large fields of my memory. This was the effect of the trauma, doctors told me. How reassuring. I would get flashbacks, for sure, but they were often vague and they didn't necessarily feel like *my* memories. My self felt like a theatre with no memory.

All the seats were empty. Nothing was happening on-stage. I sat back in my office chair and closed my eyes.

36

¶ Reg Varney, one of the university security guards whom I'd known since I was an undergraduate at Essex, woke me. It was getting really late and I had a longish drive back to the perfectly anonymous village I used to stay at on the Suffolk border. I decided to leave the last box, marked Pisces, for tomorrow. My star sign.

I got back to the little house I rented, Churchgate Cottage, next to a medieval graveyard that surrounded an undistinguished fifteenth-century parish church. The nearest grave belonged to one James Brown, deceased in 1748. Where be your funk now? I drew a very hot bath and lay there, turning things over in my mind and listening to the shipping forecast on the BBC. A repeat-loop surrealist poem:

> Dogger, Humber, German Bight. Southeast veering
> southwest 4 or 5, occasionally 6 later. Thundery showers.
> Moderate or good, occasionally poor.
> Forties, Viking. Northeast 3 or 4. Occasional rain.
> Moderate or poor.
> Rockall, Malin, Hebrides. Southwest gale 8 to storm 10,
> veering west, severe gale 9 to violent storm 11. Rain, then
> squally showers. Poor, becoming moderate.

Moderate or good, occasionally poor. Poor, becoming moderate. I lay in the steaming water and mouthed the other regions of the sea: South Iceland, Biscay, Fitzroy, Trafalgar. Bliss. It was an incantatory memory poem. Recall the sea and retain the land. 'Jeder Englander ist ein Insel.' Appropriately enough, the late night forecast was always followed by the national anthem. The islands were safe. We could all rest.

I went to bed. With the sound of automated bells in the church tower outside and the discreet aid of Ambien, I fell into a profound sleep. I immediately began to dream floridly. I was floating, small, angelic or bug-like, inside a vast Gothic cathedral. It looked like the gigantic nave of Lincoln Cathedral, but it was truly some kind of compound image of Canterbury, Norwich, Beverly Minster, Peterborough, Ely and York. I floated up to the ceiling and hovered beneath the roof bosses. I gazed from one end of the cathedral to the other. Each roof boss depicted a stage in the history of the world, from creation through the Fall and expulsion east of Eden, the figural precursors of Christ in the Kings of Israel, onwards into the nativity, the young Jesus's lecture in the blinded synagogue, the miracles, crucifixion, resurrection, ascension and, finally, Christ triumphant, in majesty framed by a vast, vagina-like mandala. His beginning is his end.

I gazed at the huge rose-shaped eastern window soaking in the hues of ruby-red glass and lapis lazuli. Then I descended abruptly into the choir, circling around the lectern in the form of an eagle – St John – and beneath the stalls. I looked intently at a long series of mercy seats or misericords each with elaborate wood carving beneath them. There was an elephant with horse's feet, a gaping-mouthed fool with his tongue stuck out, a bear being hanged by geese, a series of Jack-o'-the-Greens or Green Men peering out all phallic and menacing, a fox lecturing an audience of ducks, a blacksmith trying to put horseshoes on a dog, endless images of wrestlers, a devil conducting dentistry on a poor open-mouthed soul, and finally the image of a mild-faced mother and child dancing together.

Out I floated into the chapter house with stone carvings of three-headed kings, veiled women, fighting lions, and tumblers, directly over the dean's throne. There were many, many monkeys and the carving of a vast serpent eating a cat. The angle of a vault entered the cranium of the Green Man and went out through his mouth. There were mouths everywhere. Fiercely oral architecture. Eucharistic gluttony. Eat the bready body of God and wash it down with his sweet blood – like Leopold Bloom with a gorgonzola sandwich and a glass of Burgundy. Transubstantiation. I thought of seedcake. Back I flew into the body of the cathedral and floated there gazing at its cruciform shape, the simple vaulted ceiling and the light pouring in through the clerestory, down through the triforium into the bays beneath. I felt majestic. Then I was suddenly sucked out of the cathedral roof through an octagonal wooden lantern, my head burst through the glass and I was being pulled up into the air faster and faster. I could see the cathedral's twin towers receding below me and the vivid green flatness of the English landscape. The sky was getting deeper and deeper blue and I couldn't breathe. The skin on my face was beginning to smoulder with the intense heat. I could smell myself burning. Father can't you see?

¶ It was still dark when I woke up. Breathless and rigid with anxiety. Mouth aching from clenched teeth. I lay there waiting for light to come, listening to the BBC World Service. A show about Malian Griots. I couldn't think of anything apart from death and the vague prospect of breakfast cereal.

I drove back to the university the next morning and thought about my dream of the Gothic cathedral as a vast memory theatre. The medieval love of the figural, the dramatic and the grotesque was not, then, evidence of either some tortured sexual repression or the liberation from such repression, as we moderns arrogantly assume, but is simply a powerful and vivid aid to recollection. Before the Reformation and the rise of literacy, image rather than print was the privileged means of religious instruction. The seemingly wild imaginings of the Gothic cathedral were simply concrete ways of shaping the entirety of time, from creation to redemption, as an aid to recollection and reflection. In a cathedral, time became space, fixed in location, embodied in stone. It was a vast time capsule. Decline from Gutenberg onwards. Fuck the Reformation.

But wasn't this also true of everything, even the shipping forecast? Might not the space of a town or a city be seen as a memory theatre? One walks or moves in a city, most Bloom-like, and somehow the entirety of the past is silently whispering through locations – ghostly and sepulchral. Like a huge question mark. And implicitly that story becomes one about the future as well. The city is a spatial network of memory traces, but also a vast predictive machine.

I looked out the car window at the slow windings of the B1124 as it wended through the subtle hills of the Colne Valley and thought of the old Roman road between

Colchester and Cambridge. Traders carrying oysters wrapped in damp sacks from Mersea Island. Might not a landscape itself be seen as a memory theatre? Might not the whole globe be viewed as a set of memory traces for life, organic and inorganic, past and future? When we look at the night sky, all we see is the past; the further we look, the further back we see. To see the future, we must turn inward.

Maybe the Hegelian memory theatre is not just a map of the past, but a plan of the future, a predictive memory theatre. Everyone could have their own memory theatre. Everyone *was* their own memory theatre. If I had no memory, had I ceased to really exist at the moment of the accident? Was this a kind of death in life where I was experiencing a form of reverse dementia?

As I reached the office, the thought hit me: did Michel have plans for building a memory theatre? Or did he perhaps even build one?

¶ I opened the Pisces box. There was a compendious number of obscene epitaphs written in Latin denouncing several of Michel's academic enemies, of which one has many in France, *bien sûr*. There was also a number of translations from Martial's epigrams where Michel had crudely cut out a page of the Latin text and handwritten beside it, often illegibly, a French translation. They were awfully rude. My favourites were: 'Lesbia claims she's never laid, without good money being paid,' and 'If from the baths you hear a round of applause, Maron's prick is bound to be the cause.' Michel translated *mentula* by *queue*. 'Prick' worked quite well, I thought.

I dug deeper, through piles of notes and drafts for lectures and seminars from the final years. Among some frankly uninspiring material, I found a fascinating little presentation of Benjamin's 'The Work of Art in the Age of Mechanical Reproduction' and the beginnings of a comparison with Heidegger's 'The Origin of the Artwork'. It looked like it was dated 1997, with the word 'Pérouse' in upper case at the top of the title page, the French name for Perugia in Umbria where we met every summer for many years. There were stacks of yellowing papers which I glanced at quickly and several large Rhodia notepads with squared graph paper, as is the French custom, covered with Michel's sloping scrawl. I used to collect those notebooks and fill them with awful stretches of sub-Eliotic lyric poetry and then type them up. Thank God I stopped writing poetry.

Then, at the bottom of the box, I discovered a stack of what initially looked like unframed lithographic prints on large pieces of stiff card. On closer inspection, however, they were a series of circular charts covered with numbers, dates and masses of cramped handwriting. Each chart was arranged in concentric circles. Each circle was intersected by irregularly divided lines radiating out from the centre, which was left empty apart from some writing. Knowing Michel's predilection for astrology, I assumed they were star charts.

I felt a chill, as if someone had walked over my grave. I knew I'd stumbled onto something interesting. But the charts were impossible to read. I bundled them up with some string from my desk and decided to continue work in the university library. I needed dictionaries, reference books and magnifying devices. The librarian, Robert Butler, was an old drinking companion of mine and would be able to help.

I settled into the special collections room in the basement of the library. As the academic year had just finished, all was quiet and I was alone. It was perfect. Surrounded by hundreds of rare books on wooden shelves with a carpeted floor, all I could hear was the persistent high-pitched ringing of my tinnitus, my constant, clandestine companion since the breakdown in Nice in 1986. I began to do random internet searches on astrological charts, but my initial hunch was not confirmed. Frustrated, I called Robert to come down and tell me what he thought the diagrams were. Laconic Dundonian. He took his time with a large magnifying glass before concluding, 'They *resemble* astrological charts, drawn carefully by hand with a compass and protractor, with their concentric circles and division into what look like zodiacal houses. But they are full of words instead of the numbers, degrees, planes and lines that one would expect.' He began to peer through the glass and mouth what he saw: 'Platon, 428/427-348/347 av. J.-C... ne fait d'ailleurs référence à lui-même qu'à deux reprises dans ses deux douzaines de dialogues... Platon avait trente et un ans à la mort de Socrate... D'après Cicéron, Platon se serait éteint en train d'écrire...'

'It appears to be a biography of Plato,' Robert said. 'It recounts the few biographical facts and anecdotes associated with the broad-shouldered one, which is the meaning of Plato's name from the Attic *platys*, broad, as *platanos*, the broad-leaved plane tree under which Socrates and Phaedrus sit. You know, the *Phaedrus* takes place in the shade of the Plato-Tree.' God, Robert could be a pedant, particularly when he was right. Plato had apparently died writing. I wish I knew how he felt.

Michel had assembled all of the real or apocryphal data available about Plato, from Cicero, Hermippus, Diogenes Laertius and even Ficino, who claimed that Plato died on his birthday. (Many happy returns! There will be no returns.) He had written the data on a chart, complete with the titles of extant dialogues, several apocryphal texts for which we only have the titles, the names of purported family members (for example, Plato's brothers, Glaucon and Adeimantus, who appear as Socrates' interlocutors in the *Republic*), and some significant dates. The phone rang and Robert had to go back upstairs to resume his duties.

There was a sequence of a further ten such charts, each one devoted to a philosopher or thinker with whom Michel clearly felt a strong affinity: Zhuangzi (Chuang Tzu), Plotinus, John Scottus Eriugena, Montaigne, Campanella, Pascal, Spinoza, Hölderlin, Nietzsche and Heidegger. In short, these were Michel's favourites. The oddities on the list were Zhuangzi, whom Michel had never mentioned to me, but whose *Inner Chapters* I had read and become captivated by; and Spinoza, who initially didn't seem to fit in his canon. As with the Plato chart, the data was organized in a series of circles. In the outer circles, there was all the biographical data, information on family background, parents' occupations, education, teachers, number of children, affairs, marriages, scandals, political intrigues, etc. In the inner circle, there was a chronological listing of works, complete with one or two annotations or quotations. On the Nietzsche chart, Michel cited the final words of his final book, *Ecce Homo*, 'M'a-t-on compris? Dionysos contre le Crucifié.' It was unclear to me whether Michel, the avowed Nietzschean, perhaps finally identified more with the Crucified Christ than with the ever-playful Bacchus. Has Michel been understood? Have I?

In the bullseye centre of the circle, the date of death was marked, sometimes together with the cause and location and occasionally a short comment. In Heidegger's chart, Michel wrote, 'Le 26 mai 1976, après une nuit d'un sommeil réparateur, Heidegger s'endormit à nouveau et ne se réveilla jamais!' Clearly, he envied Martin his final night of refreshing sleep and his peaceful demise.

Michel had obviously discovered some weirdly idiosyncratic technique for plotting and recalling the lives and works of the philosophers. But then my mind cast back to Michel's essay on Hegel and to Yates's *The Art of Memory*. These were not standard astrological projections at all. They were memory maps, spatially organized devices like the memory theatres Michel had discovered in Frances Yates's book. They weren't so much birth charts as death charts, necronautical rather than genethlialogical. Their purpose was to plot the major events in a philosopher's life and then to use those events to explain their demise. Much of the script was simply illegible or had faded and many of the charts had odd, vaguely occult-like geometrical designs that resembled crayon drawings I had seen by schizophrenics when I was visiting my friend Samson in hospital after his suicide attempt (crayons were dispensed rather than pens and pencils in order to avoid suicide attempts or attacks on staff). I had no idea what the designs meant and neither did Robert.

Beneath the initial eleven memory maps, I came across another very dog-eared chart that was clearly written in a different hand. I peered hard through the magnifying glass. The chart was signed with a flourish with the name printed underneath in upper case in the traditional French fashion. It read 'Henri MONGIN' and was dated 1985. I knew that name. I wracked my brains and recalled a conversation I'd had with Anne on one of our drizzly Welsh walks. I'd asked her where Michel's interest in astrology and the occult had begun and she said that he'd learned it at the hands of one of his philosophy teachers, also an early follower of Heidegger, Henri Mongin. Clearly, Mongin had projected Michel's memory map and Michel was the inheritor of a technique that Mongin had either discovered or also inherited from a teacher. Who knows how far back this occult tradition might extend. If I could produce an heir, then maybe it would continue.

Looking more closely at the map, all the events in Michel's life were carefully recorded: his family background in Alsace, the occupation of his father, who was also a philosophy teacher in a lycée in Strasbourg, the birth of his younger brother Roger, his marriage with Anne in Rheinbeck, NY, in 1970 and so on. But the strangest thing was that the map also predicted the events of his life after the date of its composition. It mentioned his elevation to full professor at Paris XII (Créteil) in 1991 and subsequently at the Sorbonne in 1995. It also listed the titles of the books that Michel would go on to publish: *Nietzsche et la métaphysique* and *Heidegger et l'essence de l'homme*, his most impressive published work. After *La fracture de l'histoire*, from 1994, there followed an increasingly mediocre series of essay collections that finished

47

with *Par-delà le nihilisme* from 1999. It was the most productive period of his life. I remembered him excitedly saying to me in his apartment in around 1996, 'J'ai trois livres en chantier!' He had three books in production. No children were named on the map.

Michel knew that he was doomed. Did Anne know too? Is that why she left him? She saw from the map that he would have no children. Michel could see the date, time, cause and location of his death: '0421h, le 18 août 2003, La Verrière (Yvelines), crise cardiaque'. I checked the precise details with my friend Delphine in Reims, who had been a student and close friend of Michel. La Verrière was the little town to the south-west of Paris where Michel had spent his final years in a sanatorium. Knowing his fate, he had simply lost the will to live. He arrived dead just on time.

I moved more rapidly through the stack of charts with a growing sense of unease. All of the remaining maps were devoted to philosophers who had either been superiors or contemporaries of Michel or whom he had met and become curious about, such as his predecessor Sarah Kofman, Reiner Schürmann (whose name was on my office door when I arrived in New York and remained there until I left; it felt like a tomb), Emmanuel Levinas, André Schuwer, Gilles Deleuze, Dominique Janicaud, Michel Henry, and Hans-Georg Gadamer. I thought this was clearly some eccentric mark of affection. Michel had secretly designed memory maps for the philosophers he admired and had met. But that hypothesis fell to pieces with the next discoveries.

Digging deeper, I found maps for philosophers that had died since Michel's death. What was so terrifying was that all the predictions proved to be true, although Michel couldn't possibly have known that. There was a chart for his long-time acquaintance, Jacques Derrida, who died from the effects of pancreatic cancer in October 2004, four months after I first discovered his map, at the same age as his father, who had died of the same disease. Richard Rorty, whom Michel had met and befriended during his frequent visits to Paris in the early 1990s, died from the same disease as Derrida on 8 June 2007. Michel's maps seemed deadly accurate.

Six maps remained unread. I knew all the names and they were all still very much alive and a few of them were close friends of mine.[1] Mine was fourth in the pile. My throat dried, but my mind was crystal clear. I made sure I was alone. As I put the magnifying glass to my eyes, I felt strangely exhilarated rather than afraid. I also suddenly recalled very clearly when I'd met Michel in Perugia, as usual, in 1994, that he'd asked me for my birth details, exact time and place. He was very insistent about the accuracy of the information I provided. I had to call my Mum to find out (Saturday 27 February, 1960. 1500h. My Dad was at the football: LFC/YNWA). I remember saying half-jokingly to Michel: 'What, are you going to make my astrological chart?' He smiled.

I peered through the magnifying glass at my destiny. The detail was fascinating. Working through the concentric circles, I moved from briefly noted events in my life that Michel couldn't possibly have known about: my father's apprenticeship at Camel Laird shipyard in Birkenhead, his job as a sheet metal worker, my mother's

1. These individuals have been informed. After correspondence with them, it became clear that none of them was known to Michel's family which possibly explains why the boxes were sent to me in 2004. The charts are in the special collections room in the University of Essex library along with Michel's other works, but they are sealed until the time of my own death.

breast cancer in 1971, his infidelities, their divorce, the industrial accident in 1978, the names of the bands I played in, the dates of my university education, my ex-wife's name, my son's date of birth, the facts of our separation and estrangement, even the job in New York, followed by another job in the Netherlands, apparently beginning in 2009. In the inner circle was a list of works beginning with *The Ethics of Deconstruction* in 1992 and *Very Little... Almost Nothing* in 1997, both of which I had given to Michel. I don't think he read them. No matter. The list continued with perfect accuracy until 2004 and then on into the future. It appeared that I would publish a book on Wallace Stevens in 2005 (weirdly, this was already largely written); something called *Infinitely Demanding* in 2007, dedicated to my mother (I laughed); and *The Book of Dead Philosophers* in 2008 – or was it 2009? Hard to read. After that, the handwriting became nearly illegible. There was something written in German on mysticism, and then some final titles. Illegible. Did that say 'tragedy'? Maybe. There was the name *Hamlet* with a question mark beside it. I had no idea. Funny, there was no mention of the text that you are now reading.

I tried to resist looking at the centre of the circle, with the date of my death. But there it was: 'le 13 Juin, 2010, 1551h, Den Bosch, hémorragie cérébrale'. Cerebral haemorrhage. OK. I was expecting lung cancer. But where the fuck was Den Bosch?

¶ Initially, the news didn't affect me much. Rather like Wittgenstein receiving word of his terminal cancer with great relief, I found some solace in knowing exactly when I would die. I simply decided to put the whole incident out of my mind. It worked. I spent the next days packing my books and emptying my office. I met with Robert twice and was evasive when asked about the memory maps. We arranged for a small Michel Haar archive to be established at the university and I would write an introductory text for the library website. I took my memory map and a handful of Michel's manuscripts with me and returned to the gloriously suffocating heat of my first summer in New York City.

At first, everything was fine. I told no one about the map, for shame at taking seriously such superstitious nonsense. It was my dirty little secret. I decided to commit myself quietly to fulfilling my fate. It was all terribly easy. The writing of books and papers flowed in exactly the sequence that Michel had predicted without even willing them into being. I slept well. I had a series of enlivening and transient relationships. I did my job well and was popular at work. I lived contentedly in my spacious one-bedroom apartment in Cobble Hill, Brooklyn. I did a wonderful job at concealing the anxiety which unconsciously consumed me. Time passed.

In 2007, I was awarded a fellowship at the Getty Research Institute in Los Angeles and spent the year in the comfortable sterility of Brentwood, just west of the 405 Freeway, on Sunset Boulevard. I drove a silver Volkswagen Passat, had an office overlooking the Pacific Ocean, a compliant research assistant, and the use of the UCLA library. In seven months, I had written my book on how philosophers die. It was funny, full of impressively wide reading, and utterly shallow. Prior to the financial

51

collapse of 2008 and the withering of the publishing industry, I made decent money on book deals and rights
sales. Pleased with myself, I returned to New York for
another round of teaching, commitment-free relationships and vacuous socializing. I even started doing yoga.
I thought about writing a book on happiness. My new
literary agent thought it would be a great idea. Thoughts
without a thinker. Cool.

¶ In January 2008, during a bitterly cold day when it was almost too painful to inhale the winter air, a box was delivered to my place by UPS and left in the hallway. When I got back that evening, I saw that it had been sent by Barbara at Essex. It was clearly the missing box, Taurus, smaller than the others. It sat on my desk all night. A strange fear ran through me, preventing the beautifully dreamless sleep I had enjoyed since getting back from Los Angeles. I called Barbara the next morning and she said that the box had just turned up unannounced, addressed to me as before, with no letter or explanation.

I got back from work that evening around 7 p.m. and began to drink freely, staring blankly at the box. I inspected it, handling the box gingerly. Something shifted when I turned it on its side. I slit the wrapping tape very carefully with a Stanley knife and opened it. Underneath a pile of Alsatian newspapers was a circular wooden object, about a foot and half in diameter and eight inches high. The top lifted off to reveal a tiny auditorium full of painted figures on seven elevated rows with the amphitheatre divided by seven gangways. It was a maquette of Giulio Camillo's memory theatre. It was exquisite. I retrieved my copy of *The Art of Memory* and began to look at the illustrations. Was this the original model that Camillo had used to persuade the King of France to become his patron?

My landlady's family owned an antiques business, mainly importing repro stuff from Italy. Business was bad. I showed her father the theatre some days later. Any suggestion of antiquity was quickly dismissed. He disassembled the base of the theatre to reveal the carpenter's mark, the initials 'D.M.' and a date, 1986 – the year after Mongin had completed Michel's memory map. The maquette was a reproduction, probably assembled in Paris from descriptions in Yates and some drawings in the

Bibliothèque Nationale. I'd seen some of the latter in an obscure edition of Camillo that I had bought from Rudi Thoemmes Rare Books in Bristol.

The theatre sat on a table beside my bed for weeks. I liked to feel it close by. Oddly reassuring. That was when the hallucinations began. Difficult to explain. Embarrassing. I began to experience inexplicable pains in my body, something like growing pains, moving within me against my will. It made any concentration impossible. I would lie face down on the floor and feel the pain in my body move from organ to organ. Belly pain. Kidney pain. Brain pain. Lung pain. I felt like a body bag of organs. This would go on for hours.

Next, my visual perception seemed to be affected by all sorts of marginal encroachments. It felt like interference on an old-fashioned TV set. Suddenly, when walking down the street, I would see something moving or flying quickly in the far corner of my visual field. I would turn my head to look, but it was gone. Things got worse, to the point where the perceptual surface of the world began to warp and bend. It was like being in a hall of mirrors. Or in a movie adaptation of a Philip K. Dick short story. This was accompanied with a massive increase in my tinnitus and strange auditory effects, like the sound of rain, or wind, or leaves, or distant muttering voices.

A week later and I was hallucinating wildly on the subway, seeing doubles of myself or watching strange animals, reminiscent of grotesque carvings in Gothic cathedrals, float around the subway car. Were they angels? Was my body and perception being invaded by some alien force? Was God punishing me? In order to reduce the massive levels of anxiety I was feeling, I began to disengage from the world. I went into the city just twice a week to teach and returned home immediately.

Then, one evening during a lecture I was giving in early April, I experienced the most terrifying auditory hallucinations. A cacophony of voices engulfed me and then the furniture in the lecture theatre began to elevate. I became convinced that everyone in the room, including myself, was dead. I could smell my own flesh rotting. Terrified and covered in shame, I gathered my things from the office, left the building and never returned.

Alone for weeks on end, I began to think that my computer was attacking me and began to keep a careful log of events. I called it electronic harassment (EH). Here is a sample log entry transcribed from the longhand version written in pencil in order to minimize technological contact:

EH 04/17/08: 7.45 a.m. Steady heart pain at computer. 8.13 a.m. Choking shots to throat at computer from west. Sting shots to genitals same. 9.11 a.m. Seven stab shots to appendix area at computer from west. 9.16 a.m. Sneezing shots to nose at computer from west. Frenzied activity. 10.51 a.m. Seven stab shots to left side above hip at computer from east. 11.18 a.m. Intense, persistent pain attack on right side at computer from north. No pain-free moments all morning. Ache all over. 12.12 p.m. Focus on eyes at computer and in kitchen from west and south respectively. 12.15 p.m. Pulse shots to ear at computer from south. Liquid wax emission. Stab shot to left shoulder at computer from east. Next north. Teamwork. 12.19 p.m. Pulse shots to left kidney. 1.16 p.m. Lingering ache in area of left kidney from persistent deep pain attacks, mainly from east. Unable to read or write or concentrate. My body is Coventry Cathedral under German bombs. A bombsite. Melanie Klein. 3.33 p.m. Focus on eyes and genitals at computer from west. Repeated diarrhoea emission. 3.44 p.m. Nuisance itch shots to face at computer from west. Rash on the skin behind my ear. Red boils under the hairline. Diarrhoea again. 4.00 p.m. Choking throat shots at computer from west. Also deep stomach pain attack. 6.18 p.m. Stab shots to right kidney from roof terrace. Left side ache on couch from north. 8.58 p.m. Deep chest pain (heart) on couch from east. Assassins. 10.09 p.m. Strong stab shot to left shoulder from roof terrace from north. 11.35 p.m. Deep pain muscle shots from all directions. Cramps. 12.48 a.m. Brain flashes enter the repertoire. At least a dozen in bed. Profoundly disorientating. Brief bursts of painless sensation in the head, followed by disorientation. 3.48 a.m. Staggering, stumbling, occasionally falling. Toilet. Thirsty. EH log end.

¶ I went to see a psychiatrist with psychoanalytic sympathies on the Upper East Side. Expensive. Platitudinous. Useless. He suggested hospitalization and prescribed anti-psychotic drugs. At least I got an extended sick leave from my professorship and stayed at home every day. The only people I talked to were my landlady and her cat, Frances ('For by stroking him I have found out electricity/ For I perceived God's light about him both wax and fire/ For the Electrical fire is the spiritual substance...').

One insomniac night, during the usual hell of physical pain that I had got used to, I could feel something happening in my head. It felt like the loosening of a blockage, or a shifting of psychological tectonic plates. Sudden elation. The fear disappeared. An overwhelming mania washed over me. The physical pain that accompanied the hallucinations and which invaded my body were brusquely transformed. My contracted melancholic ego swelled up like a Montgolfier balloon to fill the universe. I had stopped taking the medicine days before because it just made me more miserable and robbed me of what had become my one comfort: my visions. Now they were an aurora borealis. My body was a buzzing antenna into which radio waves flooded from the entire cosmos. I was the living switchboard of the universe. My skull was a magnetized globe.

¶ Some months earlier, I had received an email from a Dutch university: Tilburg, in North Brabant. They were looking for a chair of Ethics and asked me if I'd like to be considered. What did I know about Ethics? Was I good? After finding the place on a map, I made a discovery. I told them that I could not teach full-time, but would be interested in some sort of really limited, part-time arrangement. They agreed and a contract had already been drafted. The salary was a pittance, but now that didn't matter.

I knew exactly what I had to do next.

I resigned immediately from my position in New York and refused all efforts to return phone calls and emails from the Dean's office and saw none of my colleagues. By July of that year, I left Brooklyn for good, placed my books and few belongings in storage in East New York, near JFK, and left for the Netherlands. I took the train from Schiphol airport and ninety minutes later checked into Hotel Central, in 's-Hertogenbosch, which was the full name of Den Bosch, home of the appropriately eponymous Hieronymus. It was just a ten-minute train ride from the university.

With the money I had made on the dead philosophers book, I bought a small house outside Den Bosch with a plot of land behind it, surrounded by trees. I needed some space. The house was close to an extraordinary series of sand dunes, De Loonse en Drunense Duinen, not far from the village of Vught, which was the location of a concentration camp during the Second World War – Kamp Vught – which was also the patch of heath where the entire Jewish community of Den Bosch had been burnt alive in the thirteenth century. The Germans can always be relied upon for a sense of history.

I started work on the memory theatre almost immediately. It took months to organize as I had no practical skills and spoke no Dutch. I hired a local architect called Bert van Roermund and two carpenters. Designs were drafted from Michel's maquette. I even got students from the local art school to help me make a large number of papier mâché figures, of various sizes, from six inches to two feet high, white and anonymous, looking rather like vulgar gnome-like garden ornaments. They cost a fortune and the students were incompetent, requiring constant supervision. But within three months, despite the persistent drizzle of the Brabant autumn, the exterior work of the theatre was finished. I would complete the interior alone.

The theatre was enclosed with a roof like the maquette. It stood about eight feet high and sixteen feet across. I had to stoop a little to enter through a small door into a kind of *parodos* or entrance to the left and there was the stage, elevated six inches above the ground with a simple dark wooden kitchen chair. Around me, the mini-auditorium was arranged with its seven gangways and seven tiers. The blank, expressionless eyes of forty-nine papier mâché statues stared back at me.

Then the work of memory really began. It was too cold, cramped and poorly lit to work in the theatre, so I took some of the statues into the house and began my taxonomy. In the front, with the smallest statues, I had arranged all the elements of my life that I could remember together with family attachments and friends, such as they were. The statues were brightly painted with sets of initials, number sequences and small diagrams that would bring to mind memories of my childhood, of which there weren't very many, frankly. Having my head ducked in water at nursery school. A broken arm after being thrown off a scooter. Something about brother-sister incest. By cock, she was to blame. That cunt Kevin who bullied me at school. My Ancient History teacher was called Mr Parker. Assyria and Babylon. The glory that was Greece. H. D. F. Kitto. I lost interest when we started studying medieval systems of ploughing. The accident had wiped so much clean and the rest seemed like it belonged to someone else.

On row two, I had reduced my books and papers first to a series of short summaries and from that to a series of notations and symbols, which I memorized. By learning to associate text with image through a process of lengthy training, I could flawlessly reproduce extended stretches of argument and exposition. It was amazing. I also symbolized my various plans for works that I knew I would never finish, such as my series of essays on the superiority of Euripides over the other Greek tragedians, a book called *Sartre's France*, a pamphlet on the etymologies of the names of fish in diverse languages, a set of embarrassing sub-Pessoaesque prose fragments, and a book on *Hamlet* that would now never get finished. The rest is silence.

Rows three to five were devoted to the history of philosophy. I arranged matters chronologically in a series of obvious clusters: (i) the Pre-Socratics, (ii) Platonists and Aristotelians, (iii) Skeptics, Stoics and Epicureans, (iv) Classical Chinese Philosophers, and so on. I found this remarkably easy to symbolize: a solid circle for Parmenides, a torch for Heraclitus, twin scales of justice, one inverted and the other right side up for Carneades, a line joining God and the world for Aquinas and a line separating them for Siger of Brabant, a butterfly for Zhuangzi, a snake for Plotinus and so on through the centuries. When I could, as with Copernicus (a series of circles) and Kepler (an ellipse), I made a visual note of parallel developments in physics and later in chemistry and biology. It was oddly pleasing.

And so it went on. Row five finished with visualizations of (i) Louis Althusser's theory of ideology (arrows pointed towards a head branded with a huge 'S') and his late account of the aleatory materialism of the encounter (rainfall and simple solids); (ii) Deleuze's plane of immanence as a transcendental field (a simple geometrical plane – I adapted a map of the Netherlands); and (iii) Derrida's grammatological theory of signification (a series of Chinese ideograms borrowed from Ezra Pound's *Cantos*). Row six was devoted to various personal miscellany: a series of symbolic maps registering land borders at the outbreak and end of the First and Second World Wars; the playing and coaching staff of the great Liverpool Football Club teams of the 1960s, 70s and 80s reduced to a series of initials (RH, RY, IS-J, IC, KD – YNWA); snatches of lyrics of my fifty favourite albums: from *Here Come the Warm Jets*, through *Strangeways Here We Come*, to *Fear of a Black Planet*.

Row seven was devoted to languages. French and German grammar did not present insuperable difficulties, but it was extremely hard to symbolize the complex grid pattern of Attic Greek verb forms in all three voices (active, passive and middle). By the time I had listed the relative pronouns and adjectival forms, I had almost run out of statues. I daubed the last statue with random fragments from Sophocles: 'ἄνθρωπος ἔστι πνεῦμα καὶ σκιά μόνον' and 'ἀλλ' οὐδὲν ἕρπει ψεῦδος εἰς γῆρας χρόνου'. But it didn't really matter, as I was quite delusional by this time.

By early 2010, work on the statues had finished and the theatre was complete. I installed the statues in the theatre and waited quietly for the day of my death to come: 13

June. Lucky for some. Utterly unkempt, I had no friends and kept to myself. Aside from my duties in the theatre, I spent the days on long bike rides through the dunes and developed the habit of visiting a local Trappist abbey where they brewed very strong beer. (Blond, Dubel, Tripel, Quadrupel; 1, 2, 3, 4, – I would periodically change the number sequence by which I imbibed. 1432 was a favourite. I don't know why.) I would get drunk in the afternoon and then cycle home. It guaranteed a couple of hours' sleep. To the outside eye I was a lunatic. People wouldn't return my gaze (the Dutch like to keep to themselves). But within I felt completely calm.

I'd asked Bert to design small wooden drawers to be placed under the statues, into which I put files, papers, records, photographs, and often copies of books. Although the contents of the drawers were invisible to the viewing eye and had been reduced to symbols and notation on the statues, I took solace in knowing that the objects were present. Latent content beneath the manifest. The theatre is my unconscious. Yeah, right.

Like crazy Crusoe in his island cave out of his mind for fear of cannibals, I would sit onstage and inspect my artificial kingdom, my realm, my shrunken *reál*. I sat there for hours running through the *loci* and rehearsing the meanings of the various statues until I recalled everything lucidly. Time had become space. History was geography. Everything was a map and I'd mapped everything. I'd built a vast, living, personal encyclopedia or living intelligence system, where, through mnemotechnics, I would be given a conspectus of the whole. This was the way I would finally overcome my amnesia. Total recall. Lights out.

My time of death was 3.51 in the afternoon. Every day for the months prior to my demise, I would enter the theatre and begin the process of remembering. I would sit onstage with a torch and a stock of spare Duracell batteries and begin to recollect, to inwardize the outward, *er-innern* as Hegel would have put it. Sometimes, I would begin at row seven, sometimes with row one, sometimes entirely randomly. I would shine the torch at the statue, then close my eyes and try and make manifest its meaning. I read medieval texts on the craft of memory like *The Guidonian Hand* and Hugh of St Victor's little book on building Noah's ark, *De arca Noe mystica*. The ark was within, not without. I prepared for the deluge.

My first attempts at recollection were poor. I kept forgetting and would have to look into the drawers for reminders. It sometimes took four or five hours to complete the whole sequence. It was exhausting. I began to panic. The clock was ticking. I developed a weird rash on my chest and the palms of my hands.

After a month or so of sustained effort, my technique improved and I could recall the entirety of the theatre in two hours. This was the plan: to enter the theatre at around 1.40 p.m. on 13 June, make myself comfortable, check my torch and begin the process. At the instant of my death, I would have recalled the totality of my knowledge. At the moment of termination, I would become God-like, transfigured, radiant, perfectly self-sufficient, alpha and omega.

¶ The day of my death finally arrived. The hallucinations had continued pretty much unabated since leaving New York, but became more auditory than visual. They were my only company, the only voices I heard apart from my own. Sitting up in bed at night, they would speak to me, reassure me, embolden me in a low-pitched female voice. Like a public address system in a German airport. I didn't sleep at all the night of 12 June. I took the bike out in the moonlight and looked at the dunes, the only feature in an otherwise completely flat landscape. Immanence. This commercial war and water machine of a country.

In the morning, I bathed very carefully, cleaning my feet and ears. I shaved off my grizzled beard and carefully flossed my teeth. Then I clipped my nails and tidied up the cuticles. Cuticles. I love that word. Hunger had long since left me. I felt as if my body was light and bird-like, as if I were full of air, like a medieval female Flemish mystic. Hadewych of Antwerp or Christina the Astonishing or that other one who dived into an oven and spent three days under the water in an icy river. What was she called? She lived near here. I dressed in my one remaining suit. Mortuary clothes. I seemed to need the weight of the clothes in order to prevent myself from levitating. I felt amazing, like the moment in the dream inside the cathedral all those years back. Garment of grace.

1.51 p.m. I began the process of recollection in reverse. Row seven: French, German and Greek grammar. My lips moved without effort or sound in a perfect automatism. I was like that puppet in Kleist's essay: perfection is only possible in a marionette or a God. I was somehow both. 2.30 p.m. Row five. I worked backwards through the history of philosophy. My recall was flawless: Hegel, Fichte, Schiller, Goethe, Bentham, Condorcet, Wollstonecraft. Next statue. Next statue. Next statue. Boethius, Augustine,

Gregory of Nyssa, Antony, Origen, Paul. Next statue. Backwards through the Pre-Socratics to Thales. Row two. On time. I moved through the sequence of my works. I seemed to see an arc, an idea of order for the first time, a series of lines of argument converging on a present that ascended into a kind of eternity. The philosophy of disappointment melted away into a vast and radiant immanence, like Saint Anthony at the end of Flaubert's book: *be matter*. I was matter. Matter was divine. I was God (or Spinoza). 3.26 p.m. Row one. The easiest and fastest. I gave myself the leisure to linger over certain memories and roll the words in my mouth. The first time I held my son after the emergency caesarean (where was he now? What did he do?). Touching my father's bony hand as he left for the hospice. The constant look of terror in my mother's eyes. Her hermaphrodite lover. My hand in the machine. Jilted John on the radio. Blood on the floor. Recall complete. Knowledge absolute.

3.50 p.m. The fire inside me now. My lips stopped moving. I waited. Full of Vicodin, I waited for the pain to sear through my head. I was ready. My face was relaxed. My arms hung limply at my side. The beating of my heart suddenly became irregular. It was as if I heard that woman's voice in the theatre saying, 'So, here it is at last, the distinguished and noble thing.' My eyes were open, surveying my empire and recalling everything. I felt an extraordinary lightness, a kind of beatitude that had nothing to do with happiness. An elation. An ecstasy perhaps. A feeling of absolute sovereignty. The relief at forgoing the counterfeit eternity of existence. Mortality. Now, I thought. Now.

I waited. Nothing happened. Soon it was 4 p.m. The afternoon shower that had beaten against the roof of the theatre subsided into the light tapping of drizzle and then nothing. I heard birds singing in the woods. Wood doves. Brusque return to the world. I was not dead. I began to cry. It had all seemed so perfect.

❡ I am ruined, financially. All my savings paid for the construction of the memory theatre. My teaching job is pathetic and humiliating and leaves me a couple hundred euros a month to live on. I've taken to growing my own vegetables and eating processed cheese. A diet that's easy on the teeth, which are in bad shape. Look like a Beckett character. The theatre is still there, though I haven't been back inside since that day. From the outside there is a vague smell of rotting matter. Paper and papier mâché I imagine. Mould too. I bet the local authorities come round soon to ask questions. Very Dutch.

The hallucinations disappeared back then too. I miss them. Their company. The strangest thing was that after the events of 13 June, when I woke up exhausted on the floor of the theatre late that evening covered in sweat, I became instantly consumed by a fear of death, a total grinding night-panicked terror. *Timor mortis conturbat me*. It never leaves me. It never ends. Never.

My fantasy was doubtless that I could coincide with my fate, rise up to meet it, unify freedom and necessity and extinguish myself from existence like a glorious firefly. Contingency would be abolished. It was the dream of the perfect death, the Socratic death, the philosophical death: absolute self-coincidence at the point of disappearance. Autarchy. Autonomy. Authenticity. Autism. It was a delusion of control. Death as some erection without procreation. An obsessional's garden of delights. As you can see, I am still quite the thinker at times.

Things didn't exactly work out. Maybe none of the memory maps were true. Maybe Michel just had a death wish and so did I. But it's not death that terrifies me, but life's continuation, its stretching into a distance that recedes as we try to approach. No purpose, aim or goal. That is the most difficult thing to endure. Not death, but dying. Death will happen. Yes. It is certain. Yes. But not now, and life cannot be consumed in the now. The now of nows. It is forever not now. Even if I hanged myself I would not experience a nihilating leap into the abyss, but just the rope tying me tight, ever tighter, to the existence I wanted to leave.

I didn't want total recall. I wanted to kill my memory by controlling it. Now, my memory lives and it kills me. Each man counts his rats.

I dreamed of the void, of the controlled leap into oblivion. But now everything is packed and swarming. The void has destroyed itself. Creation is its wound. We are its drops of blood. The world is the grave in which it rots.

There is a persistent rain over the Brabant heath. I see the dunes in the distance and think of rivers swelling and debouching into the vast grey North Sea.

¶ Some time passed. Years. I decided to write things down. The grotesque scale of the error I had made gradually became clearer to me. What I had built in my Dutch backyard was a flat literalization of the idea of the memory theatre. It was a sort of static, inert, dead rendering of an entity that had to be multidimensional, mobile and somehow alive. Not literal, but metaphorical. Like those guys I saw at Venizelos Airport in Athens with *metaphora* written across their backs. Memory had to be transportation. Motion. I had misunderstood history as some kind of cocktail of personal whining and the history of philosophy. This was finally dull and sad. Any life is dull when looked at in a certain light. That's why a true memory theatre has to be something else.

I went back to Yates's *Art of Memory* and reread it intensely, marking passages boldly in different coloured inks (yellow and green highlighters, red and black uni-ball vision pens). I also found a photocopy of Michel's essay on Hegel in the bag of stuff that I'd brought from New York. The brilliance of Hegel's insight was not to reduce memory to a kind of dull recitation of the past, but to create something permanently moving. A wheel that turns, returns and turns again. Hegel's memory theatre was a kind of *perpetuum mobile*, a permanently recreating and re-enacting loop. Knowledge of the Absolute, achieved through recollection, was a vast living organism, a totality endlessly creating novelty out of itself.

Everything that I had done – and Michel too with his damned memory maps – was too two-dimensional. Too flat. Like this fucking landscape. Memory is repetition. Sure. But it is repetition with a difference. It is not recitation. It is repetition that creates a felt variation in the way things appear. Repetition is what makes possible novelty. This is what Mark E. Smith meant. Memory needs to be imagintion. Transfiguration. Now, I saw it. The whole thing. An endlessly recreating, re-enacting memory mechanism. A rotating eternity. Self-generating and self-altering.

We do not make ourselves. We cannot remake ourselves through memory. Such was the fallacy driving my memory theatre. We are not self-constituting beings. We are constituted through the vast movement of history of which we are the largely quiescent effects. Sundry epiphenomena. Symptoms of a millennia-long malaise whose cause escapes us. The theatre of memory cannot be reduced to my memory. It has to reach down into the deep immemorial strata that contain the latent collective energy of the past. The dead who still fill the air with their cries. The memory theatre would have to immerse itself in the monumentally forgotten. Like a dredging machine descending down through the Lethean waters of the contemporary world into the sand, silt and sludge of the sedimented past. I had seen a machine like that once on the Essex coast. I watched it for hours. Dredging mud. The clanging noise it made. Water slipping through its metal teeth.

The problem with my memory theatre was that it was a theatre of death and it would die with me. What was the point of that? The new machine would continue forever. Forever repeating. Forever innovating. Not just the same. It would be an artifice, sure, a simulacrum, undoubtedly, but infinite and autonomous. Its autonomy, not mine. Not the same mistake again. It would be the perfect work of art. It would continue without me, in perpetuity. Endlessly. Eventually, it would be indistinguishable from life. It would become life itself.

¶ I had to begin again.

Somewhere else. Somewhere remote. This place was no good. Isolation. An island, perhaps. But which one? There are so many. Wasn't I from an island? At the very least I would need a contained environment. Somewhere small. It would involve a huge amount of work. This would not be another, static memory theatre, but a living machine whose power would be generated by the constant ebb and flow of tides. Moon powered. I began to make little drawings in crayon for a kind of cinematic projection system. I needed to find visual, moving analogues to the entirety of world history that could be projected onto a specially prepared landscape. This would be a kind of garden, but with all the trees stripped down to expose their roots and a specially prepared black grass on a series of narrow terraces that would progressively soak up the projected images. And then project them back. Paradise. But in reverse. An Eden containing all that falls. Eventually, long after my death, all the elements of world history would combine with this garden and form an artificial but living organism. I could see it very clearly. A machine that would use history to generate nature. It would be like a second fictional sun in the universe. Eventually, it would be come the true sun.

It was dawn. Light rain. Dull. I rode my bicycle into Den Bosch and waited for the local library to open. 5 a.m. Four hours to wait. I needed to consult tidal charts.

A partial glossary of possible obscurities:

A1124 — An 'A' category, single carriageway road that connects the towns of Colchester and Halstead, both in Essex.

Jean Beaufret (1907-1982) — French philosopher, notable for his prominent role in the French reception of Heidegger's thought.

James Brown (1680-1748) — citizen of Earls Colne, Essex.

Giulio Camillo Delminio (1480-1544) — Italian philosopher, known widely for his memory theatre, which was described in the posthumously published *l'Idea del Theatro*.

Tommaso Campanella (1568-1639) — Important Italian philosopher best known for his utopian treatise *The City of the Sun*.

Thomas Carlyle (1795-1881) — Hugely influential Scottish philosopher. *Sartor Resartus* (1836) is a scathing and immensely funny satire on German idealism and a fascinating philosophy of clothes.

Carneades (214-129/8 BCE) — Skeptical philosopher and head of Plato's Academy. He was known for his very loud voice.

Christina the Astonishing (1150-1224) — Christina Mirabilis from Sint-Truiden (now in Belgium), miraculously revived at her funeral and continued to perform wonders, such as levitating, surviving fire and drowning. She lived for nine weeks by drinking only the milk from her own breasts.

CHZ — *Continuously Habitable Zones* (2011), an artwork by French artist Philippe Parreno (1964-) that figures subliminally in *Memory Theatre*.

John Dee (1527-1609) — Mathematician, navigator, proponent of English expansionism, adviser to Queen Elizabeth I and Hermetic philosopher.

Dundonian — inhabitant of Dundee, Scotland.

The Fall (1976-) — A mighty pop combo from Manchester, England, led by Mark E. Smith (1957-).

Marsilio Ficino (1433-1499) — Founder of the Platonic Academy in Florence, translator into Latin of the complete works of Plato and coiner of the expression 'Platonic love'.

Robert Fludd (1574-1637) — Astrologer, mathematician and cosmologist, whose memory system may find an echo in the architecture of Shakespeare's Globe Theatre.

Frances the cat (1995-2014) — Elegant, beautiful and fastidiously small, Frances was part Oriental, part mongrel, and her good looks were a result of that fortunate combination. Born in Sydney, she emigrated to New York and liked the city. She adapted quickly, spending a number of nights on the tiles, but looked no worse for it. She could be tough on her prey, whether large pigeons, frogs, or lizards. Frances had no time for dogs, or indeed other cats. She proved that refinement is compatible with immense affection and warmth. The protagonist fuses Frances with the cat Jeoffry, the dedicatee of Christopher Smart's poem Jubilate Agno, composed during confinement for insanity in London between 1759-63.

Fulke Greville (1554-1628) — First Baron Brooke, poet, biographer of Sir Philip Sidney, adviser to Queen Elizabeth I and King James I. Stabbed to death by Ralph Heywood, his servant.

The Green Man — or Jack-o'-the-Greens, a vegetative deity, a symbol of rebirth, usually depicted as a head peering through foliage. Very often the name given to public houses in England and, by association alone, the name of an excellent brewery in Bury St. Edmunds in England: Greene King, renowned for their Abbot Ale.

Griot — West African storyteller and bardic singer.

Michel Haar (1937-2003) — French philosopher with astrological leanings. Much of what is said about him above is true. Some of it isn't.

Hadewych of Antwerp (?-1248) — Beguine visionary from Brabant, and perhaps the most profound poet of divine love.

Michel Henry (1922-2002) — An as yet under-recognized French philosopher and novelist, author of a fascinating two-volume study of Marx, a genealogy of psychoanalysis and a philosophy of Christianity. Henry was a philosopher of life conceived in terms of radical immanence and interiority.

Hermes Trismegistus — Hermes the thrice-great, who was believed to be an Egyptian priest, a contemporary of Moses and author of the Corpus Hermeticum. In the early seventeenth century, these texts were dated to no earlier than the second or third century of the Common Era, although the identity of their author remains unclear.

's-Hertogenbosch — 'The Duke's Forest', a once enormously powerful trading center from the thirteenth to the sixteenth century and home to the artist Hieronymus Bosch (1450-1516). The city's fortunes collapsed during and after the Dutch War of Independence (1568-1648). It remains a beautiful and rather haunting place.

Dominique Janicaud (1937-2002) — A French philosopher of great importance, whose work is yet to be allotted its true significance. Janicaud wrote books on Félix Ravaisson, Hegel and Heidegger as well as developing an entirely novel approach to rationality and a philosophy of time. The final work completed in his lifetime was an introduction to philosophy written for his daughter, Sophie. He was a man of great patience, good humour and refinement. He was the protagonist's maître and the person through whom he met Michel Haar.

'Jeder Englander ist ein Insel' — 'Every Englishman is an island', a saying of the German romantic poet and mining specialist Novalis (1772-1801).

Jilted John — The name of the first alter-ego of Graham Fellows (1959-), an entertainer from the north of England. 'Going Steady/ Jilted John' was released in July 1978 and reached number 4 in the UK charts. Other alter egos followed, notably John Shuttleworth, composer of the unforgettable 'Pigeons in Flight'.

H. D. F. Kitto (1897-1982) — Humphrey Davey Findley Kitto, a British classicist of great renown and author of *The Greeks* (1951) among many other works.

Sarah Kofman (1934-1994) — A prolific French philosopher, who wrote with great distinction on Freud and Nietzsche. She was appointed to a chair at the Sorbonne in 1991 and committed suicide three years later, on the 150th anniversary of Nietzsche's birth.

Martial — also known as Marcus Valerius Martialis (38/41-102/104), a Hispanic poet who lived in Rome and is remembered for his twelve volumes of epigrams, which are often very saucy and rather amusing.

Guy de Maupassant (1850-1893) — French writer and acknowledged master of the short story form. His 1887 story 'Le Horla' is a work of unforgettable terror. Please read it.

Metrodorus (145 BCE-70 BCE) — From the town of Skepsis in ancient Mysia, in Anatolia. He was known for his prodigious memory and his hatred of the Romans.

Pico della Mirandola (1463-1494) — Student of Ficino and philosophical meteor whose syncretic metaphysics drew on a dazzling array of sources, some of them Hermetic, Zoroastrian, Orphic, Pythagorean and Cabbalistic. He ran into trouble with the Pope and died in suspicious circumstances, possibly poisoned by his secretary.

Henri Mongin — As far as I am aware, he did not exist.

Pethidine — A once popular opioid of the phenylpiperidine class, for the treatment of acute pain, whose effects are often compared with morphine.

Necronaut — a term derived from the Greek for 'corpse' or 'dead' (*nekros*) and sailor (*nautes*) to describe a being concerned with navigation and mortality. It also describes a member of the International Necronautical Society, founded in 1999 in London. Such members are legion.

Clément Rosset (1939-) — A French philosopher and author of many, short, scintillating books, notably *The Real and Its Double* and *Joyful Cruelty*. A joyfully tragic thinker whom the protagonist encountered at the University of Nice, teaching ancient Greek and Roman materialism.

Bert van Roermund (1947-) — Actually not an architect, but a Dutch legal philosopher and professor at Tilburg University.

André Schuwer (1916-1995) — A Dutch philosopher who taught at Duquesne University, he was ordained as a Franciscan priest in 1943. A proponent of phenomenology, especially Husserl and Heidegger, and a person of great wit and kindness.

Siger of Brabant (1240-1284) — The most radical of the Paris Averroists, who proposed the separation of the truths of philosophy, as articulated by Aristotle (who else?), from the experience of faith. After being forced to flee Paris for sanctuary in Orvieto, Italy, he was stabbed to death by his secretary.

Simonides of Ceos (556 BCE-468 BCE) — Greek poet, noted for his lyrics, elegaics and epigrams, and inventor of the mnemonic technique behind the idea of the memory theatre.

Sophocles — the great Attic tragedian who needs no gloss, but here are translations of the two fragments quoted above: 1: 'A man is nothing but breath and shadow.' 2: 'But no falsehood lasts into old age.'

Rudi Thoemmes — purveyor of rare books concerned with the history of ideas. Based in Bristol, England.

Tilburg — A peculiarly ordinary, indeed rather plain, city in the southern Netherlands. It was once famous for its manufacture of woollen goods.

Timor mortis conturbat me — 'The fear of death confounds me,' a repeated refrain in a beautiful poem by the Scottish poet, William Dunbar (1460-?) called 'Lament for the Makars'.

La Trappe — A highly intoxicating Trappist beer fabricated in several varieties in De Koningshoeven Brewery, Netherlands.

University of Essex — Established in 1963, Essex is a small, architecturally brutal, but once intellectually beautiful and vibrant place. The protagonist in *Memory Theatre* had been an undergraduate and PhD student before becoming a teacher in the Philosophy Department. He left in 2003.

Frances Yates (1899-1981) — Dame Frances Amelia Yates was an English historian of great distinction who taught and researched for many years at the Warburg Institute of the University of London. In addition to *The Art of Memory* (1966), her major works include *Giordano Bruno and the Hermetic Tradition* (1964) and *The Rosicrucian Enlightenment* (1972). Although what is sometimes termed 'The Yates paradigm' has been contested, for example by Paolo Rossi in *Logic and the Art of Memory* (1983, first published in 1960) for exaggerating the 'occultism' and 'Jungianism' of the mnemotechnic systems she studied, Rossi goes on to conclude, 'Dame Fraces Yates was not only a scholar of the highest level, she was also an extraordinary person'. The protagonist would concur with this judgement.

YNWA — 'You'll Never Walk Alone', a show tune by Rodgers and Hammerstein from *Carousel* (1945). It became the club song and anthem of Liverpool Football Club (est. 1892) after the release of a 1963 cover of the song by Merseyside band, Gerry and the Pacemakers. The song has been known to move grown men to tears.

Zhuangzi or Chuang Tzu (369 BCE-286 BCE) — The philosophically most interesting and linguistically unsettling of the classical Chinese thinkers. His book, also called Zhuangzi, is composed around a core of seven 'Inner Chapters' and is a principal source of Daoism. The core idea is that everything should be allowed to behave in line with its nature, which is consistent with the notion of *wu wei* or 'non-action', which does not mean doing nothing but only doing that which accords with the way in which a thing truly is. Do nothing and leave nothing undone.

Viglius Zuichemus (1507-1577) — the Latin name of Wigle Aytta van Zwichem, a Dutch statesman and jurist of great intellectual renown who held powerful political position in the Netherlands and was a friend of Erasmus.

Acknowledgements

The author would like to thank the following people:
Jacques Testard, his editor, for the audacity of inventing a
new press in order to house this little book and producing it
so impeccably; Nemonie Craven, his agent, for her constant
support and for believing in this piece of writing when he
didn't; Dan Frank, for some brilliant structural advice which
allowed him to rethink and rewrite the whole project; Tom
McCarthy, for loosening his tongue; Hari Kunzru, Lisabeth
During, Avital Ronell and Leo Hollis for helpful words;
Jamieson Webster, for enduring his tiresome neuroses without murdering him yet.

Fitzcarraldo Editions
8-12 Creekside
London, SE8 3DX
United Kingdom

ISBN 978-0-9929747-1-8

Design by Ray O'Meara
Typeset in Fitzcarraldo
Printed and bound by TJ Books

fitzcarraldoeditions.com

Fitzcarraldo Editions